∞

Progress in Divine Union

Also by Raoul Plus
from Sophia Institute Press®:

How to Pray Always

Winning Souls for Christ

Raoul Plus, S.J.

150

Progress in Divine Union

SOPHIA INSTITUTE PRESS®
Manchester, New Hampshire

This translation from the French by Sr. Mary Bertille and Sr. Mary St. Thomas of *Progress in Divine Union* was originally published by Frederick Pustet Co., New York, 1941. This 2004 edition by Sophia Institute Press® contains minor editorial revisions to the original text.

Copyright © 2004 Sophia Institute Press®

Printed in the United States of America

All rights reserved

Cover design by Theodore Schluenderfritz

On the cover: Gentile da Fabriano (1385-1427), *Saint Francis Receiving the Stigmata* (Fondazione Magnani Rocca, Corte di Mamiano, Italy). Photo courtesy of Scala / Art Resource, New York.

No part of this book may be reproduced, stored in a retrieval system, or transmitted in any form, or by any means, electronic, mechanical, photocopying, or otherwise, without the prior written permission of the publisher, except by a reviewer, who may quote brief passages in a review.

Sophia Institute Press®
Box 5284, Manchester, NH 03108
1-800-888-9344
www.sophiainstitute.com

Library of Congress Cataloging-in-Publication Data

Plus, Raoul, 1882-1958.
    Progress in divine union / Raoul Plus. — [Rev. ed.].
        p. cm.
    Includes bibliographical references.
    ISBN 1-928832-82-2 (pbk. : alk. paper)
    1. Mystical union. 2. Spiritual life — Catholic Church.
3. Prayer — Catholic Church. I. Title.
BX2350.3.P58 2004
248.4'82 — dc22   2004008871

04 05 06 07 08 09 10 9 8 7 6 5 4 3 2 1

To Mary,
Queen of Saints

Editor's note: The biblical quotations in the following pages are taken from the Douay-Rheims edition of the Old and New Testaments. Where applicable, quotations have been cross-referenced with the differing names and enumeration in the Revised Standard Version, using the following symbol: (RSV =).

∞

Contents

Part Two
Develop a spirit of prayer

∞

Introduction

∞

*Respond to
Christ's call*

∞

Adversity, which easily discourages weak souls, strangely enough incites strong souls to greater perfection. They understand that troublesome times, even more than peaceful times, demand the complete gift of self. It is to help courageous souls that these pages are written. The thought is not new, but a deeper penetration of it may be helpful.

We need saints now more than ever before!

But how does one become a saint?

There are but two means, and both are essential: to be willing to consider self as nothing, to practice a life of complete generosity in which all is for God without any reservation or let-down; and to strive for intimate union with God, for recollection or the spirit of prayer — a life of prayer insofar as circumstances and the duties of one's state permit.

There are only two mountains in the world: Thabor and Calvary. On Thabor we pray in secret, heart-to-heart with God, and unite ourselves with His infinite Majesty.

Thabor's prayer, however, is not necessarily one of ecstatic joy; for our sanctification is difficult, and often enough it is only the hard road of Calvary that brings us to Thabor. On Calvary we suffer with Christ crucified, but our divine Savior, ever eager to reward those who follow Him that far, will often transform our Calvary for some days, or at least for a few hours, into Thabor.

When our Lord has found enough generous souls to whom this program is not a hard saying, but rather an inspiring challenge impelling them to accept both its immediate difficulties and threatening hardships, you may be sure that through them, or at least because of them, He will complete the work of redemption.

Administrators, politicians, and those charged with governing our temporal welfare must do their best. Their effort alone, however, will not raise the world's ruins and restore life to the world. If the work of reconstruction is to be fruitful and effective, we must have devout souls who are willing to consecrate themselves to a deeply spiritual life.

We face a challenge!

Christ awaits our answer!

Let it be understood: God has no place for triflers or merely curious onlookers. The redemption of the world is no trifling matter. The world is bought at a great price!

Respond to Christ's call

We do not all have the same talent to offer. God asks much of those who have much, but from the less gifted He is content with the widow's mite; this meager offering is by no means less valuable or less effective. Each one must give his all, and this all varies greatly in quantity and quality. The duty to win back the world does not devolve upon religious alone, even though the demands made upon them are naturally greater. The field is open in the world to the married or single, the youth, the mature, and the old.

Everyone is invited. No one is excluded.

> *Lord, You know my weakness.*
> *Nevertheless, I dare to ask You*
> *to enlist me among Your workers.*
> *You can count on me.*
> *But if You only knew*
> *how much I count on You!*
> *We two!*

∞

Progress in Divine Union

Part One

∽

Strive to
overcome your self

Chapter One

∾

Develop a
broader vision

∞

Either we have or have not committed grave sins. Whatever the case may be, the necessity for self-conquest confronts us.

Even though we have never sinned grievously, the fact still remains that we entered life burdened with Original Sin and its consequent evil tendencies arising from the triple concupiscence: concupiscence of the eyes, concupiscence of the flesh, and concupiscence of the mind. The Blessed Virgin Mary alone, through her Immaculate Conception, was preserved from this taint and, as the Holy Church teaches, was given in addition to her fundamental preservation the precious grace to keep free of actual sin throughout her life.

These formal definitions of the Church bring us to the double realization that from our birth we have within us a tendency that, if not guarded against, leads to catastrophe; and further, that at no moment are we free from a possible head-on collision with temptation. Who can be certain that his moral brakes will not play him false sometime or another? Like autos with defective brakes on a difficult road, we need to be on our guard for every turn or slightest grade.

Someone has said that civilization does not consist in gas, electricity, railroads, and airplanes, but in organization and struggle against Original Sin. The truth of that statement is plainly evident.

"Man is not good by nature," observed Jacques Rivière. "His nurse knows that." And again he says, "The dogma of Original Sin is a fundamental consideration for a sane and truly just estimate of man."

In the light of this truth, how absurd and presumptuous is Rousseau's theory that man is totally good and in consequence has nothing to fear from himself. This ridiculous theory, however, has been sufficiently exploded. How grateful we should be to the Church for giving us a true conception of our human nature!

But without accepting the fundamental axioms of a deceptive and confusing secularism, do we not reason, in practice at least, as if an evil concupiscence did not exist and as if we had not to fear its possible treachery?

Nothing is more characteristic of the present age than its utter disregard of the virtue of prudence. One reads everything, exposes himself to everything, takes any risk, and boasts of his ability to pass more or less unscathed through extremely dangerous situations.

Even souls most desirous of practicing virtue are not exempt from delusion. Sometimes priests whose mission it is to guide souls are somewhat set against those spiritual principles that extol the necessity of self-conquest. Forgetting that there are definite stages in the ascent to God, and that even souls far advanced in virtue are not for that reason preserved from temptations, they become apostles of easy spirituality: "Leave to the old ascetics their taste for sacrifice; we need more modern methods. Love God much, and everything else will come to you!"

Truly, love is the foundation of all that is worthwhile. We will speak of it later, and let us hope, more worthily; for we may not forget that real love demands sacrifice and virility. Further, to find its fulfillment, it must be surrounded by a healthful protection and by clearly defined bounds, solidly guarded. Our hearts should resemble the divine Master's: a burning center of love protected by a crown of thorns.

Those who know have pointed out how forgetfulness of sacrifice affects the destinies of nations. Souls are like nations; if they do not take heed to their security, it will be seriously compromised. *Vigilate!* Watch! *Confortamini!* Be brave!

If we have sinned, the necessity for self-conquest is greater. The soul must struggle under the weight of its willful transgressions in addition to the burden of its original concupiscence, because our acts follow us. They do not, of course, follow us to the extent of suppressing our liberty or of enslaving us, but they do facilitate subsequent falls of the same nature.

Everyone knows the psychology of habit. The commission of an act, either good or bad, renders more facile its repetition. Try to use a paper or a piece of material that you have once folded; both will automatically fall into the same folds unless you prevent them.

Now, our souls are still more pliant and more readily affected. Nothing is lost on them; everything leaves some impression.

How important, then, is education, which should develop a bent for the good! How baleful our sinful acts, which are not only disobedience to God and cause for chastisement, but also a destructive force leading us to a later renewal of our defection.

In the face of this truth, what well-meaning person would deny or fail to understand the value, or better still, the necessity of an intensive training in sacrifice as a wise preservative for the sacred treasures of the soul?

Msgr. d'Hulst, an excellent psychologist and eminent theologian, who was in no way an extremist, but who saw clearly the needs of souls, did not hesitate to say during a retreat he preached in 1891 at Notre Dame of Paris, "I know that I shall astonish more than one by presenting mortification as essential for salvation. It is in fashion to consider it an extravagant virtue that might well be left to the perfect."

Then he explained that the words of our Lord, "Whoever does not deny himself cannot be my disciple"[1] are meant for all, when they refer to necessary self-denial — an essential means or condition that must be adopted if one wishes to avoid sin.

Taken in their strictest sense, the words of the divine Master point directly to maximum generosity. In this sense, one cannot pretend that they concern all men. "But in their broader interpretation," as Msgr. d'Hulst said, "they retain their universal application; they remain the absolute rule for every human life that wants to adjust its principles in accord with its destiny."

[1] Cf. Luke 14:27.

11

It is clear, then, that a truly spiritual book will be above all a *manual of combat*. For, in the most advanced life of perfection as well as in the most elementary ascetical life, the struggle against self is indispensable.

Most of our faults spring from the same source. Each has his peculiar temperament, his tendencies. There are the fiery and the phlegmatic, the cheerful and the gloomy, the sanguine and the nervous, the slow and the active, the healthy and the sick, the energetic and the soft, the self-contained and the emotional, the imaginative and the unimaginative — an indefinite medley, and in each category a thousand variations.

Our failings crystallize according to a certain form that is generally the same in like temperaments. This is a point deserving close attention. It is up to every individual to know himself and to struggle along the lines of a well-planned strategy.

The particular examen is a precious weapon in this combat. It should not, however, be put on a parallel with prayer; paying attention to oneself is certainly not equivalent to paying attention to God. But for the majority of souls, both activities are useful. They are, so to speak, centrifugal and centripetal. Prayer makes us go out of ourselves to center in God and is by far the superior exercise;

examen makes us enter into ourselves, not to find ourselves, but to help us make place for God, and that, too, is exceedingly worthwhile. It is evidently necessary at the beginning of the spiritual life, and afterwards, generally continues to be fruitful.

We will not dwell upon this point any longer except for this final remark: Is it not perhaps because they too lightly esteemed the particular examen that some souls who are considered very holy, and are doubtless so, do not overcome certain glaring failures, for example, against charity or humility? It is very well to lose ourselves in God, but we also ought to refrain from unkindness in dealing with our neighbor, from inordinate manifestation of our ego, and from our too-ready flare-up of impatience. Prayer certainly; but also self-control.

Even among souls who have rid themselves of conspicuous faults, there still remains a certain strain of lightness, an inability to look at life with a large view, a general tendency to be narrow and one-sided. How one would like to find in certain noble and holy persons greater liberty of spirit and broader vision!

Fr. Faber speaks somewhere of "the depths of frivolity that we carry about in us," which, according to him is, of all subjects touching upon our salvation, one of tremendous importance. Cast a glance over the things that attract us or amuse us, or hold our attention, or interest us as relaxation or subject matter for conversation. What a disarming childishness is ours! To think that when we have such aptitude for the great, we are dominated by the small, allowing trivialities to engross us!

You have no more faults to correct? Then turn your attention to this: develop a broader vision not only when you are before God in prayer, but also when confronted by the meannesses of life. Never add any meanness of your own!

Try to be watchful in this regard. You will find that it is not useless.

Chapter Two

Atone for your sins

∞

Self-preservation pertains to the present and the future, but there is a past. If there have been some transgressions in the past, right order demands that compensation be made.

In every fault there is a twofold element: a greater or lesser injury to God by our disobedience to His will, and the seizing of a pleasure to which we had no right. With sincere repentance, the state of disobedience ceases; but the stolen pleasure deserves a corresponding penalty; otherwise, theoretically speaking, there would be an advantage in having sinned: peace would be re-established with God, and at the same time, one would have had the benefit, however slight, of the stolen pleasure. This touches upon the fundamental idea commanding the virtue of sacrifice or, more specifically, the virtue of penance.

When one offends God, he immediately creates an indebtedness that must be settled by either a self-inflicted chastisement or a punishment imposed by divine justice.

This makes clear the need for Purgatory. If one dies repentant and in God's grace, but without having atoned either by willing acceptance of life's sufferings or by voluntarily imposed sacrifices for his stolen pleasures or sin, the soul must be detained in a place of purification. He is in God's grace. God loves him. But because he has not made complete satisfaction, the sufferings of Purgatory are necessary. If the sinner refuses to repent, death fixes him definitively in his state of revolt — in Hell. Here his suffering effects no remission, since he has willfully accepted separation forever from God.

Let us return to a consideration of that which more immediately concerns our earthly life. The same day that sin entered the world through Adam's perverted will, the necessity of suffering came into the world. St. Paul said, "The wages of sin is death,"[2] and the sinister accompaniment of death is suffering.

God, in His mercy, permits suffering here below to enable us to make up for our failures. Instead of rebelling against suffering, we ought to consider it a true blessing. In the event that the suffering imposed by divine providence is not sufficient for complete atonement, God, in

[2] Rom. 6:23.

His mercy, accepts our self-imposed penance to complete the satisfaction for faults committed in this life.

Perhaps someone will say, "I have committed only very slight faults. Are not the sufferings of my life more than enough to expiate my minor transgressions?" Yes, and no doubt, it is again God's great mercy that He uses this means to exempt us from Purgatory so that after death we may go directly to Heaven without any need for further reparation.

We never know how much will be required by way of satisfaction for the unjustified pleasures we seek on earth by transgressing the divine precepts. Besides, in speaking of sacrifices, it must be remembered that they need not be always of our own choice. As our first and foremost means of victory over self, we should seize those myriad opportunities that are offered to us to resist temptation, to correspond to the inspirations of grace, and to accept cheerfully whatever suffering may come to us.

All spiritual writers are agreed that the sacrifices enjoined by providence are more efficacious than those of our own choice, provided, of course, we accept them with a supernatural intention. Likewise crosses sent by God are more purifying, and because there is less of self in them, their merit is often greater.

Further, God shows His greatest mercy in permitting us to receive more trials than is necessary to expiate our personal sins in order that we may make satisfaction for the sins of others. Moreover, there are fervent souls who, having been able by grace to forego all excesses, need no self-imposed penances. They are inspired by God to follow faithfully the way of sacrifice, so that through them the treasury of the Communion of Saints may be filled and superabundant reparation may be made.

This touches upon one of the greatest marvels of our divine religion — namely, that all can act for all, that each individual can merit for others, and that if we can make reparation for ourselves, we can also make reparation for those who could not or would not make entire satisfaction for their own sins, whether they are already in Purgatory or still struggling in the Church Militant.

Sacrifice, then, is offered in atonement not only for one's own sins, but for the sins of all; not only from a motive of personal interest, but of common or social interest. We shall treat of this in another way and at more length when we speak of suffering as a means of sharing with Christ the work of redemption.

To many, *sacrifice* means only corporal austerities. The body's part in sacrifice, however, is merely sequential. Sin consists essentially in a digression of the will. Mortification will be, then, essentially a sacrifice of the will, an interior act of virtue: the faithful submission of the will to the least wishes and designs of God, even though this submission makes exacting demands on our self-love, our egotism, and our caprices. Because the body and the senses often cause our defections of the will, interior mortification — and it should always be interior — ought to be accompanied by exterior mortification. For this very purpose we have the penances of fast and abstinence imposed by the Church.

Chapter Three

∞

Carry your
cross with Christ

∽

Over and above the motives of preservation and expiation which are based on a justifiable self-interest, we as Christians, especially if we would be fervent Christians, have a stronger and nobler motivation for the spirit of sacrifice. It is love that urges us to imitate Christ, to carry like Him and after Him, in our soul and in our flesh, the marks of the Crucifixion.

As soon as the baptized child can make a Christian gesture and can lisp a prayer, he is taught to make the Sign of the Cross. Someone guides his untrained hands in tracing upon his weak and tiny person the symbol of redemption.

Later he will learn that the Cross demands more than a gesture from time to time; that the disciple of a crucified Master cannot evade crucifixion. Not that nails will tear his hands and feet, nor thorns pierce his brow, but that in the spirit of the gospel, he must fulfill the instruction of our Lord: "If any man will come after me, let him deny himself"[3] — deny himself at least to the point of avoiding sin, especially serious sin, and of practicing the essential duties and virtues of a Christian.

Fervent souls will not only have at heart what is strictly necessary, even though that in itself constitutes a sizable program, but they will seek to identify themselves, according to the degree of their generosity, with Christ, who sets the example.

Perhaps in their inexperience, they will seek for a time to serve God generously, avoiding the cross as much as possible. That is what St. Margaret Mary[4] did. Early in life, she resolved to serve God in the way of perfection, but fearing the cross, she took pleasure in paging through the lives of the saints to discover a model who, although wholly consecrated to God, was still not given to great self-abnegation. It is not hard to guess how she was repaid for her curiosity: sanctity without mortification does not exist.

Fortunately Margaret Mary did not abandon her resolve. Whoever wills the end wills the means. She took

[3] Matt. 16:24.

[4] St. Margaret Mary Alacoque (1647-1690), Visitation nun who received revelations of and promoted devotion to the Sacred Heart of Jesus.

her share of the means so well that later, when asked to choose between reproducing the image of Christ resplendent in glory with no trace of suffering and Christ covered with wounds, she extended her hands in a gesture of intense love toward Jesus suffering.

Princess Elizabeth of Hungary,[5] when but a child, was so overcome one day in church at the sight of the crucifix above the high altar that she removed her diadem. Adorned with a crown of jewels, she was ashamed to look upon the bleeding Christ crowned with thorns.

It is easy to understand how, in youth especially, a noble heart can be eager for the cross and the mortified life the cross exacts. But with many, is it not a spurt of enthusiasm? A fine flame while it lasts, but it dies out little by little as it comes into contact with the vicissitudes of life or with the mere monotony of repeated demands. It is only too easy to prove that inconstancy is a characteristic of the majority.

It takes no little courage, surely, to enter upon the religious life; and the novitiate leavens the soul to rich

[5] St. Elizabeth of Hungary (1207-1231), daughter of King Andreas II of Hungary, niece of St. Hedwig, and widow who became a third order Franciscan.

promise. What a disappointment, then, to see one soul after another collapse and fall, after a surprisingly short time. Apparently the action of the leaven is weakened because the substance is too heavy to be penetrated. Where lives of complete renunciation could be expected, there is mere existence and a minimum of abnegation — no grave defection, of course, but sluggish tepidity, little cowardices, and stagnation.

What is true of many priests and religious is equally true, if not more so, of many Christians living in the world. There have been many brave beginnings. One dreams of widespread and deep apostolic gains; another enters upon marriage with the hope of leading a saintly life. But, sooner or later, lassitude settles upon the soul, difficulties arise, and the individual comes to a standstill or completely renounces the most beautiful part of his program for life. How cruelly unstable our lives! How frequent our desertion of good resolutions!

If we were to question the majority of Christians really striving after perfection on their manner of practicing in spirit and in truth our Lord's instruction, "the violent bear it away"[6] — that is, only those capable of doing violence

[6] Matt. 11:12.

to themselves are worthy of the kingdom of Heaven — how many could say that they have taken it seriously? Nevertheless this injunction given in the Gospels was not for the little group of Apostles alone, but for the whole crowd.

To what extent does my life, which is supposedly Christian, deserve to be called a life of violence — violence to my selfishness, violence to the enticements of the world, violence to the demands of the flesh, violence to the seductions of the Devil? Does violence really characterize the life of the majority of good Christians?

Pursuit of comfort, pleasure, and ease is the motivating force of almost every phase of present-day life, even among those who aim at a Christian life; every possible concession is made to reconcile the demands of caprice and the most fundamental exigencies of the Faith — the gospel and the world; the cross and comfort; the least possible sacrifice and the greatest possible ease.

Oh, excuses are not wanting!

We may sometimes say, "Are we obliged to aim so high?"

But what do we mean by "so high"?

We must aim at the perfection God expects of us. Could the Gospel still be called the Gospel if it were stripped of one of its strongest precepts: "Whosoever doth not carry his cross, and come after me, cannot be my disciple"?[7]

Or again, we may explain that we began but could not continue. Perhaps our idea of our duty was too idealistic, too fantastic, unable to stand up under the test of practice. Or, we may have abandoned our first fervor through simple cowardice. St. John pronounces an anathema against those who, although called to a higher life, abandon their beautiful ideals through want of courage, thus bungling their lives.

We may never forget that holiness consists in repeatedly beginning over.

Our Lord, our divine Leader, fell on the way to Calvary. That is significant. If the cross becomes so heavy for us, His disciples, that we let it fall along the road, do we take it up again to follow the path to the heights that beckon us on? Or do we give way to discouragement, forgetting what Fr. Faber says: "Many holy and heroic lives can be described as an entanglement of generous beginnings"?

Sometimes we count too much on our own strength; then God must show us our folly through the evidence of facts before we can accomplish anything.

[7] Luke 14:27.

Sometimes we prefer a false humility to the necessity of being heroic. We give vent to our feelings in prayer similar to that which Jacques Rivière one day addressed to our Lord: "My God, take from me the temptation of holiness. Be satisfied with a pure and patient life which I shall do my best to offer you. Do not deprive me of the delightful joys which I have known, which I have loved so much, and which I yearn to possess again. Do not be mistaken. I am not of the stuff from which saints are made. Do not tempt me with impossible things. Do not lead me on to unbearable sufferings."

Upon whom can God count, then, if He cannot count on us? Surely, this is a hard saying. The invitation is austere. Christ says: "I count upon your courage and upon my grace which will help you. That is the truth. Will you also go away?"

God asks a beautiful service, a rigorous service: militancy, the cross, self-denial, and violence. We would betray our Lord were we to soften these words of the Gospel.

But let us not forget these other revealed words: "My yoke is sweet and my burden light."[8]

8 Matt. 11:30.

We lack courage because we lack love. Let us contemplate the Cross with new eyes: "Look," our Lord tells us, "Was it easy for me? I persevered because I love you. It is true that in the Garden of Olives I begged the Father for a time to remove the chalice, but when I realized that I was asked to drink the chalice to the last drop, I pronounced my *fiat* and accepted all. Imitate me. We shall help each other. Your cross is heavy; mine was heavier, far heavier than yours. Be willing to take up your cross again. I shall be your Cyrenean."

"What, my Lord, You have reversed our roles? I ought to come to help You, and You take up my burden?"

"Yes, my child, I know you. You are weak; I know that. But you have not given up yet, have you? We shall join our efforts, and together, we shall invoke Mary. She knows how to reach the heights. She awaits us both there. Let us not give up before the hour of our *Consummatum est*."[9]

---

[9] "It is finished" (John 19:30).

Chapter Four

∞

Imitate Christ's
spirit of sacrifice

∞

The motive to imitate Christ is indeed very noble; it is not, however, the noblest height to which we may aspire. The essence of Christianity consists, if we have grasped the spirit of the gospel, in our identification with the divine Vine itself under the title of members of the Living Vine: the Christian is an extension of Christ, as the branch of the tree is an extension of the tree.

It is not enough, however, to look upon the features of Christ and try to reproduce merely the exterior traits of the divine Model, as a student might copy the canvas of a Master. More than that is required. We constitute an integral part of the whole Christ, and we must continue Christ by interior virtue.

Christ came upon earth to repair sin, but who is Christ — *the whole Christ?*

On Calvary, our Lord offered Himself to His Father as a sacrifice for the world, and burying us deep in His gaping wounds, He engrafted us into His body — into that unique Vine stretched upon the blood-drenched trellis of the Cross. We were, since the Fall of Adam, such wild branches. The whole Christ is, then, not only the personal Christ who lived in Judea and who lives now in Heaven and in the Eucharist, but also all whom He has "Christ-ed," all whom He has made one with Himself, all who through this marvelous engrafting are called to live His life with Him, with His Father, and with the Holy Spirit.

The whole Savior is, furthermore, our Lord plus ourselves, the members of Christ; Jesus the Son of Mary, the Child of the Father, and all who are privileged to be cells in the Body of Christ. Since we are identified with His person, we are identified with His work. The Redemption is the work of Christ, the work of the whole Christ.

This truth ought to change our usual way of thinking. Most of us passively assume that Christ has done everything, that we are concerned in the Redemption only insofar as we have benefitted by it. We are not even aware of the importance of our active duties: that we are also redeemers with a definite work to carry out in the salvation of the world.

Holy Mother Church does not pretend that our part in the Redemption is the same as our Lord's. The merits of the divine Head are, according to theologians, merits of strict justice or of strict equivalence; as members of Christ, our merits are congruous merits, merits of fitness or decency. In other words, the mediation of Christ alone is more than sufficient to save a million worlds; our mediation is efficacious only because our Lord wanted it. He made us one with Him just to make this collaboration possible, but from the moment Christ willed this collaboration, it became an obligation for us. If, as members of Christ, we refuse or forget to contribute our share to Christ, the Head, something will be wanting in the Redemption.

Consider, then, our true grandeur in its full light. Redemption is the work of both the Head and the members; it is a cooperative. If the world is not saved or sanctified as it should be, we cannot blame Christ, for surely He has done His part; the fault lies with the members who, unmindful of their duty, neglect to fill up what is wanting in the Passion of Christ. It is no small matter to have been made members of Christ.

Furthermore, we can be saviors of the world with Christ only if we are like Christ. What means did Christ choose to redeem the world? He chose sacrifice. Without shedding of blood, there is no remission. Christ prayed for us, He gave us His precepts confirmed by His example, and above all, He gave His blood. Of the three apostolates prayer, action, and suffering, the most efficacious is suffering. That is why St. Paul, who could have said, "I complete what is wanting in the Redemption of Jesus Christ," preferred the highest and said, "I now rejoice in my sufferings for you and fill up those things that are wanting of the sufferings of Christ."[10]

Our duty is evident. The work of redemption is binding upon both the Master and the disciples; the manner of redemption chosen by the Master must be adopted by the disciple. To be a Christian is to be not only one redeemed but also a redeemer, not only one saved but a savior. What nonsense, then, to refuse sacrifice!

The doctrine of the Mystical Body gives us the most convincing proof for the necessity of abnegation and renunciation in a truly Christian life. Even if we had never sinned and were not conjointly liable for the sin of Adam, we would be called to Christian sacrifice because, as members of Jesus Christ, we must participate actively in the work of redemption.

The tremendous implications of this doctrine can be seen readily. It is primarily the love of our Savior that

[10]Cf. Col. 1:24.

urges us on to sacrifice, but that love includes the members of Christ, because *catholic* means all-embracing. To love the whole Christ is the only genuine Catholicism. Devotion to Christ finds its counterpart in devotion to our neighbor. These two loves, that which is directed toward God and that which is directed toward our neighbor, are inseparable; inseparable are the two commandments that sum up the whole law and unite in one love: "Thou shalt love the Lord. . . . This is the greatest and first commandment. The second is like to this: thou shalt love thy neighbor as thyself."[11] This is the fulfillment of our Savior's doctrine.

For some, the thought of our Lord will dominate; for others, the thought of souls. Often the two points of view unite in one and are mutually enriched.

In other spiritual books, for instance *The Folly of the Cross* and *The Ideal of Reparation*, we have shown how the understanding of Christian dogma has produced through the ages and especially in our times a rich garner of souls who have dedicated themselves to the life of a victim in union with Jesus, the great Victim. In the Holy Sacrifice of the Mass, the oblation of Christ, the divine Head and

[11] Matt. 22:37-39.

the oblation of the members are united in one immolation for all the immediate intentions of redemption.

We ought to have a clear understanding of what the dogma of the Mystical Body permits and even commands in our particular circumstances of life. Once we are convinced of our duty, we should go to the limit in our Christ-life. We are not here merely to serve God and save our own souls: we are bound to save our neighbor. This point is important. How can anyone work effectively for the salvation and sanctification of his neighbor unless he uses the most saving and most sanctifying means: sacrifice?

Chapter Five

*Give all so that you
may receive all from God*

∞

Some practical considerations may have been slighted by treating primarily of the doctrinal motives requiring the spirit of sacrifice. A few supplementary reflections, therefore, are necessary.

Our first concern as souls aspiring to divine union, and consequently living, or striving to live, in the state of grace, is not preservation from sin. Aware, however, of the dangers of temptation, we will take no chances, but be always vigilant in guarding our senses, especially the eyes. Even if living in the world, we will avoid as far as possible pagan comforts and mundane superficiality with its cloying frivolity.

Further, we will be impelled to offer ourselves as victims of reparation, not because we have so many personal sins to expiate, but because our keen realization of the sins of the world is for us, as for our Lord, a crushing agony.

Above all, we will recognize ourselves as living continuations of Christ. We will be convinced that we must do more than imitate His gestures; we must adopt as our rule of life that which was the very soul of Christ: the desire to fulfill perfectly the Father's will, which is the complete abandonment of our own will:

I no longer live. It is not I: I do not count.

If this is what You want, I shall do it.

It is high perfection to act always as Christ would act. It means complete abnegation of self.

As living members of Christ, we will be conscious of our part in redemption. We are by vocation instruments of redemption. How many saving crosses can be offered by souls united with the Cross of Christ! There are first of all the trials common to all — those that weigh upon the entire world, a country, a particular social class, or a family; those that afflict the individual, morally or physically: failure, poor health, spiritual aridity; their number is legion. Trials often proceed from one's profession: one, like Louis Veuillot, is crucified to his pen; another to his desk or to his store or business; another will find it trying to live in celibacy or widowhood; another will be tied down to a home with dependents to support, children to rear, and a thousand cares to claim his time and energy. Besides all these, there are the crosses that come from necessary fidelity to the laws of God and the Church. Then there remains a wide and holy margin for the generous sacrifices of each individual.

Instead of focusing our attention solely on what we must give, let us consider what God gives us in return for the little we can do: His all in comparison with our all — those little nothings that our love offers and that His love appreciates as though they were truly something.

St. John of the Cross[12] gives in plain terms what God expects of us. According to St. John, we must take all or leave all. We receive nothing for nothing or All for all. That explains why so few are willing to take up the Cross.

The question of the extent to which God can communicate Himself to us brings us to the second consideration of this book, the spirit of prayer.

[12]St. John of the Cross (1542-1591), Spanish Carmelite, mystic, and reformer of the Carmelite Order.

Part Two

∞

Develop a
spirit of prayer

Chapter Six

*Be attentive to God's
presence in your soul*

∞

Every soul in the state of grace is the dwelling place of the Most High. But does every soul live in its own dwelling — live there with God? The doctrine of sanctifying grace assures us that God lives in us, but how many of us live in ourselves? Our Lord enters His dwelling, and do we not often leave Him there waiting alone and in coldness?

This is the whole problem of recollection: to dwell where God dwells. It is the great secret, simple, clear, and within the reach of everyone. It is not always convenient to go to church, especially if the church is at a considerable distance.

To enter into ourselves, however, is no laborious pilgrimage: from our exterior self to the intimacy of our soul is not a great distance. We are at the very door of the cathedral. In fact, there is no door; we have merely to raise the screen of our languid inertia.

"The Master is come! Tell him that I am at home. I want Him. I want His presence."

Progress in Divine Union

We must work together in perfect harmony. God dwells in our soul, and we unite ourselves with Him there. Faith teaches us the truth of the divine indwelling, and through the spirit of Faith, we accustom ourselves to participate actively in this inner life of the soul. It is a matter not of establishing the doctrine, but of living it — not of proving it, but of capitalizing on it. Much less is it a matter of imagining a pure fantasy as something real, but of grasping the reality as something vital.

Let this magnificent reality function in our lives.

Chapter Seven

Pray attentively, with your heart and your will

∽

As souls aspiring to recollection, we must give place to prayer in our lives insofar as the duties of our state permit. If we aspire to easy contact with God, we must train ourselves to deliberate contact with Him. Our Lord does not give Himself unless we seek Him; to possess the precious treasure, we must pay the price. God may occasionally grant moments of intimate union to those who do not seek Him, but ordinarily not. The desire to receive God's special attention in prayer presupposes the willingness to recollect ourselves. If we do not open our hands, we will not receive the gift. Prayer opens the hands and the heart.

A few good-willed but ultramodern authors have proposed, contrary to the best masters of the spiritual life, that since mental prayer is essential to religious life, it should not be insisted upon for laypeople and secular priests.

These authors overlook entirely the fact that the priesthood derives its excellence primarily from the eucharistic power of Christ. They claim, in treating of secular priests, that the perfection of their state resides in their participation in the pastoral power of the bishop, that is, in the most excellent exercise of the virtue of charity. According to them, the virtue of charity for the neighbor manifests itself in works of zeal. In preparing a sermon or course of studies, or visiting the sick, the parish priest works as much at his own sanctification as he would during mental prayer. Prayer is a good and desirable exercise, they agree, but it is far from having the indispensable efficacy claimed by spiritual writers, who, for the most part, are religious writers. We cannot but feel that priests who reason thus will hardly be apostles of prayer to the souls they guide; they have never experienced the sovereign importance of mental prayer, in fact, they themselves claim to find no doctrinal justification for mental prayer.

Is not a decline in the desire for thoughtful prayer to be feared, especially at this time, when, more than ever before, we need prayerful souls among the clergy and laymen?

Where, if not in prayer, will the priests and likewise the supposedly fervent and apostolic faithful nourish their zeal? Could the advice St. Bernard[13] gave to his former monk, Pope Eugenius III, have lost its import: "Do not be

[13] St. Bernard of Clairvaux (1090-1153), abbot and Doctor.

satisfied with being a canal; be a reservoir. Acquire for yourself first what you distribute to others"? Alas! Does not everyday experience give undeniable proof that if so much beautiful zeal of both priest and layman is fruitless in many cases, it is not for lack of apostolic endeavor, but because the spirit of prayer is wanting?

These overzealous souls want to be canals, but they forget to draw upon the divine Source before attempting to give to others. They give much, but it produces nothing. One thing is wanting: more time spent with God in prayer. First contemplate, remain quiet in prayer; and then go to souls. This was the procedure of all the great apostles: Paul, Francis Xavier,[14] the Curé of Ars,[15] and Fr. Chevrier. No one can deliberately go against the regular order of things without sooner or later being the loser. Furthermore, the Church, ever solicitous for the welfare of souls, has always, and even very recently in regard to activism, opposed those who stress exaggeratedly the so-called active virtues to the detriment of what they speak of disparagingly as the passive virtues. One would almost

[14]St. Francis Xavier (1506-1552), Jesuit missionary to the East Indies.

[15]St. John Vianney (1786-1859), patron saint of parish priests; known as the Curé of Ars.

be tempted to say, "Less zeal and more prayer." A devouring zeal is dangerous if it consumes the time the apostle should spend with God in prayer.

Although what has just been said is of importance, we have no intention of presenting here a treatise on prayer, but will merely give a few practical suggestions.

Prayer usually requires preparation. If we had an audience with the Holy Father, we would not say, "I will get along all right when I get there. I will take a chance on it." A minimum of common sense and courtesy would demand that we reflect thoughtfully on the subject of our interview. The Holy Father may take the initiative in conversation; if not, we can have recourse to our selected topics.

Sometimes we are extremely impertinent. We are perfectly willing to receive — oh yes, to receive — but seldom think of *preparing* ourselves to receive. By dwelling in us, God has already taken the lead, and still we expect Him to do everything, to overwhelm us with consolation without any effort on our part. Always on the alert to receive, we never even so much as think of contributing our share. We ought to endeavor to have at least a suitable method of procedure and a proper esteem for prayer.

The choice of possible considerations or subject matter does not constitute prayer. It is only the prelude. It is however necessary, unless God deigns to let us lose ourselves in Him without any effort on our part. This is a rare and extraordinary privilege reserved for those who have devoted themselves to prayer for so long a time that they live constantly in the presence of God. For them there is no perceptible transition from their habitual state of recollection to their recollection at prayer.

Neither are we praying when we mentally run through proposed considerations or read an inspiring text. Reflection is not prayer, and much less is reading. We pray only when there is a lifting of the soul to God, a movement of the heart and an act of the will. However useful and even necessary reading and reflection may be to arouse the heart and to move the will, they are only preliminaries. Prayer calls for a united effort of the heart and the will. We pray only when we make acts of virtue, whether of faith, of hope, of love, of humility, of adoration, of thanksgiving, or of petition. Prayer is defined as a lifting of the soul to God to adore, to thank, to ask pardon, and to make known our needs. The higher the virtue's place in the hierarchy of virtues, the more noble the quality of the prayer. Of all the acts mentioned, love is the most sublime, the one that brings about intimate union and that, like the others, can lead to a state of virtue.

To occupy our minds with a great multiplicity of acts at prayer is a mistake. Souls accustomed to ready contact with God may find themselves, in a comparatively short time, established in a fixed state requiring neither variety, diversity, nor change. We must follow the Holy Spirit, not hamper His activity. If, for example, He deigns to fix us in a disposition of intimate union, we can only yield to His designs. Great sorrow and great admiration express themselves in silence. In the grip of profound experience, inward activity is intense but not manifold; it is rather a unified activity. It would be unwise to disturb the silence or trouble the union by an untimely interruption.

Prayer does not require a multiplicity of acts; it may thrive best on silence. We too often think praying means speaking to God. It is rather listening to God, especially for souls eager for union with Him. We are all great talkers; that is true in dealing with our fellowmen and much more so in dealing with God. Time spent in silence with God is not lost. Magdalen was far from idle when she contemplated our Lord in loving, silent adoration.[16] Words are not the best medium of expression for intimate union; words are powerless in great depths of emotion. The Word

[16]Luke 10:39.

Incarnate came to earth when all was enveloped in silence;[17] He has not changed His ways since that solemn midnight. Silence is still His divine aureole, the surest sign of His presence.

St. Ignatius[18] advises that when ideas, pictures, and words have served their purpose, when by means of them we have arrived at the heart of the ineffable, there is only one thing to do: to taste interiorly. Taste, as it is used here, is not necessarily taken in its literal sense. *Taste* as St. Ignatius and the best spiritual masters use it, means to penetrate interiorly, and according to Cardinal Newman,[19] to relish, to go to the very marrow, to experience in one's whole being the reality considered: the greatness of God, the immensity of His love, the infinite mercy of our Savior, the immaculate purity of Mary, the expiatory or redemptive power of suffering, the incomparable price of life, or the splendor of death.

The enlightenment received in prayer will not necessarily be new. It consists more often in a deeper and more

[17] Cf. Wisd. 18:14-15.

[18] St. Ignatius of Loyola (1491-1556), founder of the Jesuit Order; known for his *Spiritual Exercises*.

[19] Ven. John Henry Newman (1801-1890), churchman, scholar, and convert to Catholicism.

striking discovery of a familiar truth. To have known is one thing, and then to discover that we really did not know is quite another. It would be difficult to define precisely what the enlightenment is. It is not usually a question of vision or intellectual understanding. It is rather in the realm of another sense, a sort of mysterious touch, a definite and at the same time vague impression, a contact, a feeling, a taste perception; and this last includes the idea of interior relish. The enlightenment will usually be in the realm of taste, not necessarily sensible, but sometimes, at least, partially sensible. At other times, it will be purely spiritual and may occasionally be accompanied by a certain dryness. It is a kind of manna in a desert. No other nourishment is comparable to it. But what a nourishment it is in the midst of total absence of everything, in complete solitude, far away from everything, where we seem even to be far from God, so well do we realize that God is infinitely different!

Because the nourishment is from Heaven, the interior joy is boundless and entirely beyond the senses. Because the nourishment reminds us that God is infinitely distant, the distress is unspeakable! Something so good and yet so strangely bitter. It comes from Heaven, but it is not Heaven. In truth, what a torment this earth is! We think we are approaching God, but in reality we are approaching only the consciousness of how infinitely far God is from us. Bliss and torture: and torture more often than bliss. Hunger is satiated; but thirst is increased.

At times, everything is dim and diffused. In the case of physical taste, a delightful sensation may be produced either by virtue of the vivid keenness of perception or by the variety of stimuli offered. Sometimes, too, the spiritual flourishes in sensible delights, although this is not the highest type of union. Or it may happen that our souls experience no sensible joy. We hold our ground and remain at our post; we continue our arid march in the desert with no perceptible consolation. Not even a drop of water or a taste of manna is granted. The union is purely of the will — an austere union that is perhaps the strongest of all; a union that demands great courage and which God reserves for virile souls. How many of us give up prayer when deprived of consolation! We dream of Thabor and find Calvary! The prie-dieu is our place of crucifixion.

Instead of attempting to distinguish between the workings of ordinary grace of the Holy Spirit and that of extraordinary grace in the intimate history of the soul, let us put forth all our effort and give God free scope. Theorists must necessarily differentiate, and their classifications are useful to spiritual directors in recognizing the various states of prayer.

One thing alone is important in prayer: to love with all our love, to press on without making any attempt to look back over the road we have traveled. Anything that might alter this singleness of purpose would devitalize the absolute purity and simplicity of our ardor.

The masters of the spiritual life have treated adequately the method to follow in either aridity or distraction. We will merely remark here that many distractions could be eliminated if the soul fostered habitual recollection. In spite of every precaution, however, it remains true that we are all endowed with sensibility and imagination, some more strongly than others.

It will often happen that because we are deeply engrossed in our work, the preoccupations of our daily life accompany us to the threshold of prayer and sometimes far beyond. To love is to will to love. To pray is to will to commune with God. But our peace must not be disturbed if, after having done all in our power, we find that our mind still rambles and never succeeds in fixing itself on anything. We can have recourse to vocal prayer, to the contemplation of a crucifix or a picture, and occasionally to writing, but all must be done peacefully.

Await patiently and perseveringly God's hour. Prayer is not a telephone conversation; the Most High does not have to answer as soon as we pick up the receiver. To know how to wait, after working for all we are worth, is the secret of gaining generous responses. But why even think of pay — and yet, one beam of light or a slight degree of union will liberally reward the efforts of the long watches during which God seems to be dead.

Finally, some of us may contend that we are satisfied with vocal prayer; that we never have had any success with mental prayer. Vocal prayer, however, is not enough for a truly prayerful life, and this admits of few exceptions. The whole soul enters into meditation; there is, as we noted before, something deep and unifying in it. In many cases, words are only a substitute for thought; they stifle it rather than reveal it. The answer of the saintly Curé of Ars: "I look at Him, and He looks at me," gives us a clue to the proper attitude before the Blessed Sacrament and reveals the incomparable character of intimate communication without the medium of another's thought such as is found in a prayer book.

When we go to visit a friend, we do not take with us a manual of conversation. A child's best New Year's wish is not one he has copied from a book, but one that springs spontaneously from his filial affection even if his language be ever so faulty.

The words of another rarely express adequately our own thoughts and sentiments. It may be what we want to say, but we would express it differently. Personal prayer derives its value from that ineffable character, that certain something which belongs to us alone and in which a friend discovers our best self.

We may object that the prayers and Liturgy of the Church are the best prayers of all and therefore sufficient. Assuredly, of all vocal prayers, the official prayers of the Church are to be preferred. We must not forget, though, that their value as prayer is derived from their intrinsic meaning.

Prayer, even the official prayer of the Church, is prayer only if it is a cry of the soul, if it comes from the heart. It is earnestly recommended to monks who chant the Office and to priests who recite it to meditate frequently on its hymns and psalms in order to guard against a parrot-like recitation. Every vocal prayer, however noble it may be, is considered prayer only insofar as it is mental prayer. This holds true for the breviary, the Mass prayers, the Hail Mary, and the Rosary. The mere recitation of words upon words does not give glory to God; the intention alone gives the glory. Because of the intention God accepts the prayer, in spite of its emptiness, as an elevation of the soul. This is prayer in its lowest form.

The familiar story of the priest who said, "I have finished my breviary. Now let's pray," is not so much a joke as we think; it expresses a rather ordinary attitude.

St. Teresa of Avila[20] gives the most conclusive estimation of the matter in the twenty-third chapter of *The Way of Perfection*: "The essential factor of mental prayer is not silent prayer; if in vocal prayer, my whole soul is occupied with God, if I keep myself reverently in His presence and give more attention to this than to the words I pronounce, I combine in this act mental prayer and vocal prayer."

But, she adds with gentle irony, "how anyone can pretend to be praying if, while saying the Our Father, his mind is filled with worldly interests, is beyond me."

Some may hold that many of our meditations are not real prayer. The fault, then, does not lie in mental prayer itself, but in the use we make of it. The deficiency is rather subjective than objective; it is not in the intrinsic quality

[20]St. Teresa of Avila (1515-1582), Spanish Carmelite nun, mystic, and Doctor.

of the prayer, but in the incompetence of the person meditating.

Vocal prayer is surely not to be scorned. If it is made well and in the manner just presented, it is the best preparation for effective mental prayer. In our first attempts to meditate, we are not so much in need of words to stimulate reflection as of formulas to express our thoughts and feelings; since our own expressions are inadequate, we may find ready-made prayers very helpful. Besides, as we have already said, the value of the prayer depends upon the meditation that accompanies it. Words are merely words; beautiful words may be given out by a victrola, but a victrola has no soul. Prayer is an expression of the soul. The little Shepherd of Chablais, to whom Francis de Sales[21] taught the Our Father, and who found so much meaning in the first word that he could never get beyond it, glorified God more by lingering on the one word than he would have by reciting thoughtlessly an endless number of Our Fathers.

Although the Church, knowing she was dealing with a very large public, proposed only formal prayers in the Liturgy without officially requiring interior recollection, she

[21]St. Francis de Sales (1567-1622), Bishop of Geneva.

intended, nevertheless, that interior recollection should accompany the formal prayers. When favoring personal prayer, whether in religious institutes or in Catholic centers, or when approving masters of the spiritual life who advise personal prayer, Holy Mother Church proves that she does not consider liturgical prayer as the only kind. Practically all the confidences God has entrusted to His saints were revealed, not during Office, but during private prayer.

Is it not said of our Lord in the Gospel that although He was assiduous in the observances of the official public worship, He often withdrew from the crowd to pray interiorly? In addition to the great sacerdotal prayer of the Last Supper, the first outline of the Liturgy, our Lord gave many private prayers and the divine counsel: "When thou shalt pray, enter into thy chamber . . . and pray to thy Father in secret; and thy Father who seeth in secret will repay thee."[22] Let us take the Gospel in its entirety.

For many of us, vocal prayer serves as a support for mental prayer; without the repetition of the Hail Mary of the Rosary, we would forget the mystery. Our powers of attention need a rallying point. Certain individuals, for

[22] Matt. 6:6.

example, are more united to God while engaged in manual work in which their hands are occupied and their minds free, than if they were wholly unoccupied. This type of occupation could be found in knitting or embroidery work, or in the routine kitchen duties that the cook can fulfill without natural overeagerness, and with all her attention riveted on God. If idle, such individuals would become the prey of distractions or sleep.

All rules, however general they may be, still admit of exceptions. Each one must know what method of prayer is best suited to his own needs. Often souls accustomed to mental prayer and eager for union with God will prefer a vocal prayer to a text offering definite points of meditation. We cannot refrain from quoting again the great contemplative St. Teresa of Avila:

> I know several persons whom God has led from simple vocal prayer to sublime contemplation. One among them could use nothing but vocal prayer. She became so distracted when she attempted mental prayer that she could not endure it; she recited the Our Father several times while thinking of the mysteries of the Passion and thus entered into intimate union with our Lord. She came to me one day

greatly distressed that she could not make a mental prayer or devote herself to contemplation. I asked her what prayers she recited, and I realized that while merely saying the Our Father she entered into such high contemplation that our Lord raised her to divine union.

Always tactful and adept in dealing with love, St. Teresa answered her, "That is all very true. Do not worry. Recite your vocal prayers with as much purity of intention and attention as you are capable."

It remains true that there are exceptions to the general rule, and kinds of prayer that may be held as vastly different and widely separated in books and in theory will, at times, be found closely related in actual life. Rules are rules, but the supreme rule is that God leads souls as He wills.

Chapter Eight

∞

Develop union with
God through prayer

∽

Fidelity during the hours of prayer engenders an almost natural facility in prayer at other times. While this is not its only advantage, it is one that is valuable and easy to understand.

The very act of forcing ourselves to spend generously at the feet of God the moments that our life, if intelligently planned, allots to prayer, brings us during that time to a degree of intimate divine union. Were this the only result, our gain would be immense. If, in conversation with a sincere friend, we find enrichment, how much more we can expect from converse with our Friend above all friends.

Prayer brings into view new horizons of thought. When we have been absorbed in a divine atmosphere for some time — and let us hope that this time is never grudgingly given — our whole being becomes penetrated with the divine: our intellect dwells on the supernatural, our feelings are caught up by the supernatural, and our imagination fixes itself on the supernatural. Little by little, the super-natural becomes the normal atmosphere of our soul. God, Christ, and the Blessed Virgin are no longer mere names but living personalities. The presence of the Holy Trinity in the depths of our soul, the life of the Savior in the Host, the marvel of the immense and fruitful communion of souls in the state of grace, are no longer nebulous theories but vital realities. The kingdom of God, which our Lord told us is within, is no longer an accessory in our life, but it *is* our very life.

"First things first, and all other things in their place," becomes our principle, with the result that all the human affairs of everyday existence assume their proper place, which is by far not the first. Our soul accustoms itself to live in truth, that is, in the divine. Our feet rest solidly on the earth but our conversation, that is, the whole tenor of our life, is in Heaven. The supernatural takes precedence over the natural. Our efforts to approach divine realities constrain divine realities to respond, and by the normal workings of habit, they begin to control us, to dominate us. If one tries often and for long periods to adapt himself to a certain climate, he will eventually feel as if the cli-mate has adapted itself to him, becoming a part of his existence.

Develop union with God through prayer

We are all familiar with the expression "master an idea"; it would be much better to say, "Be mastered by an idea." Prayer achieves this for us. It establishes union with God not only while we pray, but makes this union relatively easy for us, in keeping with our character and occupations, even when we are not explicitly occupied with prayer.

Consider again a conversation with a friend. Once the conversation has ended, the contact is not broken; it is less lively, perhaps, less real, more diffuse, but effective still. Multiple memories arise: the words spoken, the dear face, the continued sense of the happiness of being together. Our friend has gone and yet remains. No one else sees him, but we never cease seeing him, and all that we do, we do in the light of his invisible presence, just as a young wife finds her whole house brightened by her husband even when he is away at work.

When we deal with our divine Friend, the supernatural action of grace cooperates with the normal and human workings of habit. God never allows Himself to be outdone in generosity. He seeks those who seek Him. He pursues with His attentions the soul that places its happiness in loving Him or at least puts forth effort to give Him, whenever it can, a proof of love. When we exert ourselves in prayer to think only of Him, He comes to us in the midst of our occupations. That is characteristic of the Holy Spirit. He is magnificently grateful, reciprocating a hundredfold every little attention we pay Him.

Of course, it is true, as was suggested before, that our occupations, some of which are so absorbing, our disposition and temperament frequently so unstable, our imagination and feelings constantly active, are sometimes helps and very often hindrances to these divine contacts, these occasional and fleeting communications. But the law holds: to pray sometimes helps to pray often; nothing more readily develops the spirit of prayer than prayer; nothing so impels God to unite Himself to us at every moment as our resolute effort to meet Him at fixed times for prayerful repose close to His Heart. We must not expect God to make all the advances; we, too, must expend some effort.

Before we try to arrive at an intelligent understanding of what this effort means, we will give some thought to the meaning of prayer. Our "elevation toward God," which is prayer, can take place in three ways. In its weakest form, it consists simply in being in the state of grace. According to many authors, all acts placed when this fundamental state of union exists and the soul possesses divine life can justifiably be called prayer.

Develop union with God through prayer

Others claim that to have prayer, in the strict sense of the word, there must be in addition to the fundamental state of grace an intention of elevation toward God. This intention can be actual or virtual. It is actual if formulated at the moment one starts to act: "My God, I offer You this work," whether the words be said explicitly or implied by an equivalent act. It is virtual if it has been formulated at a time considerably antecedent to the beginning of the act it elevates to God. For example, in the morning on arising we can direct to the Most High through the Morning Offering, or any other formula, all the activity of the day. Then, as the hours and minutes roll by, the various actions rise in homage to God. We may, too, from time to time throughout the day, think of raising our mind and heart to God. At the time we make these intentions, the Morning Offering, and the other periodic offerings, they are clearly actual; their effect of "elevation" governs virtually the length of time that follows until the next actual intention. In this way, strong states and weak states follow upon one another to constitute a continuous and almost constant elevation of the soul.

What we would like to stress here is the manner of making the good intention as constantly actual as possible. We know that "to pray always" does not command us to a state of constant actual elevation exclusively, and that the majority of souls united to God live rather in a state of virtual elevation. Our Lord does not require continuous acts of union that, we might say, are for the most part impossible, but a continuous state of offering. In other words, God asks not so much for constant attention to Him as for the constant intention to do nothing that is not wholly for Him.

We will not rest satisfied with a virtual intention only, but seek to attain a union with God that is morally constant and actual. We say morally constant, because, clearly, aside from special graces, our capacity for attention, even when wisely and consistently disciplined, is too weak and our occupations in many instances are too distracting to permit the twin effort necessary to think at one and the same time of what we are doing and of God, for whom we work. There will consequently always be something of the actual and of the virtual in our intentions. Our problem resolves itself to this: How can we foster a progressive supremacy of the actual intention?

We ought to begin early in the morning. Someone asked St. John Vianney for advice on how to remain united with God at every moment. The saint responded by revealing what he did himself: "At the beginning of the day, I try to unite myself closely to our Lord, and then I act with the thought of that union."

There is, indeed, a favorable discipline of thought that has many advantages. Among spiritual masters, St. Ignatius notably suggests it: In the evening, as soon as we no longer have to deal with others, we ought to establish ourselves in a sort of "great silence." Then, having prepared the subject of prayer for the next morning, we should exercise vigilance over our thoughts so that nothing extraneous to the subject chosen enters in. Further, we should endeavor to fall asleep thinking of God, and should our sleep be broken, try even then to avoid the admission of any distracting ideas. Upon arising, before we allow the preoccupations of the day to engross us, we ought to make a gentle but firm effort to fix ourselves in God. This is of tremendous importance if the hour of prayer follows close upon the hour of arising. Night gives us a free, clear mind; since the last movement of our soul before going to sleep was supernatural, it is fitting that we oppose any intrusion of distracting ideas that might trouble us at prayer. If, for some reason, the time for prayer must be set for later in the day, as is often the case with the mother of a family, it is no less important, since very often all depends upon a good start.

A lively recollection of the divine presence within us, or of approaching Holy Communion; the thought of the sanctification of our day, which will help to make up the immense ensemble of the life of souls; the gripping realization of prayer needed for sinners and of reparation to be offered for the world for its sins of the night that has passed; the feast of the day, if the Liturgy holds a special appeal — any such thought will establish contact with God. We must use what best succeeds for us. But it must be something definite, strong, truly stimulating, and expressed with a maximum of love. The warmer the air and the stronger the wind, the higher the balloon rises. It is a question, we must not forget, of elevation.

To unite ourselves to God is first and foremost a supernatural act. We must, then, earnestly beg from Heaven the necessary help that the Lord may multiply His advances and that we may have the quiet of soul and the required courage to correspond to His interior solicitations. We must pray humbly and persistently, convinced that alone, without God's powerful grace, we shall fail.

In the spiritual diary of young Lyautey, the following significant entry was found under the date of October 1876, at which time the future marshal, then twenty-two, was taking an officer's course at Saint Cyr: "You think you are holy; you really believe you are worth something because I have flooded you with graces. . . . But what have you done? You have never struggled."

How well his ideas bring out the truths we considered in the preceding chapter! The meditation continues in a similar strain:

Without ceasing, I have sent you my inspirations as I am giving them to you now at this moment; without ceasing, I have allowed you to be recollected, and you have never known how to make use of my revelations. I have left you because your pride repelled me. Instead of recognizing that it was I who deigned to speak to you, you persisted in believing that in your fruitful reflections it was you who elevated yourself above your life through your own generous efforts, and looking upon yourself with admiration, you became self-complacent.

How can you hope to meditate with profit when, instead of withdrawing from yourself, of establishing silence in your soul, you become, as it were, two persons, the one prostrate before the other; the one seeming to pray while the other extols him saying, 'You are great; you are noble; you are holy; you are generous.' Even now as I speak to you, are you not inclined to admire yourself because you are attentive to me?

Think, then, my son, of all those to whom I do not speak at all. Think of the absolutely special graces you have received.

What wisdom in this young officer's meditation! We so readily believe that of ourselves we are capable of something. Should it happen that we enjoy consolations, we imagine that these divine favors are the reward of our goodwill. The failure of many of our efforts toward union with God can be laid to our secret pride.

To get a good start in the morning, through the energy of one's love and the help of the precautions taken the evening before; to renew quietly the bonds of divine union at favorable opportunities, such as on entering a room, hearing a bell ring, taking leave of someone, or beginning or finishing a piece of work; to ask God humbly for the desired help to correspond to grace: these are all positive helps to union with God. They offer possibilities for achievement that will be more or less easy according to the alertness and aptness of the individual soul. Above all, in one who is inclined to give a little more time to prayer and well-chosen spiritual readings, they ought to have appreciable results.

There are, further, certain negative precautions that are important: the avoidance of useless thoughts and the curbing of natural impetuosity.

We all have the habit of conversing with ourselves, and nothing is more fruitful if the ideas exchanged are worthwhile. Unfortunately, if we are not vigilant, we become for the most part the victim of useless prattling, as harmful as the chatter of two persons who continue to talk when they have nothing to say.

St. Francis de Sales once jokingly spoke in praise of poor memories, quoting in this connection the words of St. Paul to the Philippians: "Forgetting the things which are behind," and he showed the spiritual advantage in not remembering so many things when we are occupied in prayer or the concerns of our daily life.

"We never live," a certain philosopher once remarked. "We hope to live." It might be good to add that not only do we project our thoughts into the future, but we unceasingly scrutinize the past. Truly, a weak memory can sometimes be very profitable, for have not many of our failings and nearly all of our inattention to God come from the play of our memories, in season and out of season?

Furthermore, certain natures are the prey of impressions: they react to everything, for everything, for nothing. They laboriously concoct dreams throughout the day. They build up imaginary situations, one more fantastic than the other. They probe the thoughts of such and such a person. Upon the slenderest hint, they invent a whole novel. From a single word they overheard, they deduce a whole argument, arriving at positive conclusions. They are living kaleidoscopes. Women are said to be particularly adept in this kind of sport. They are affectionate, and that may strangely enough be a help in prayer; they have impressionable souls and an imagination that easily rambles, and that can be very detrimental to recollection.

What can we do? Each of us must discipline himself, using the means at hand. We must go to God by means of the possibilities that are ours. The abilities of one are not the abilities of another. Even when we have a definite set of fixed rules, we must always in practice take account of the personal coefficient. God knows that well and does not require of all a like achievement. The essential thing is that we go to the limit of our grace, not to the limit of another's grace. That is the reason for the wide diversity among the saints, even among souls dwelling together in the same institute or in the same family. Nothing is more delightful than this variety in the different types of religious psychology.

The great model of interior silence is the Blessed Virgin. She lived on supernatural realities alone; other things did not count. She kept the divine in her heart; the human remained at the door and could gain no entrance.

Among its advantages, cloistered life, by favoring exterior silence, disposes the soul to interior silence which in principle becomes easy. That is no reason for individuals called to live in the world to imagine that they are at too great a disadvantage. One can even in the cloister abandon himself to a really distracted life and neglect almost completely the interior life, while a married person given to absorbing work in business or in the management of a household may keep closely united to God. It is not so much a matter of setting as of soul. One can be very silent, that is, interiorly silent, in the midst of talking, and talkative in the midst of silence. The problem is one of discipline — discipline of the imagination, discipline of the feelings.

It is perfectly legitimate to desire to know much. Happy the one who is eager for every new enrichment and whose mental antennae are keenly sensitive. But how much useless curiosity there is! Likewise how many love to talk for the sake of talking; love to see for the sake of seeing. What a triumph of levity and vagrancy!

"But," we may object, "we never know when such and such curiosity, apparently useless, may have rich fruit." Let us not be pharisaical, but use common sense. We are speaking here of that curiosity which we can clearly recognize as vain. In regard to that, let us be inflexible. Just as we will have to render an account of every idle word — and few think of this, judging by the many indiscreet profaners of silence — so, too, will we have to render an account of every manifestation of idle curiosity. And that does not only mean curiosity in regard to evil, but also curiosity in regard to worthless trivialities. Do we or do we not desire union with God? If we do, then why this playing around?

We may, of course, on occasion allow ourselves, by way of relaxation, some flights of fancy and may think or dream to our delight. The bow suffers from being always taut; it must be loosened at times. What we must not condone is a habitual let-go attitude and a lack of self-mastery and self-possession.

To the discipline of our imagination, our feelings, and our curiosity we must add the discipline of our activity. We are dying from too much activity. We must understand, of course, that we need not withhold the fruitful expenditure of our energy and the judicious use of our strength in the work confided to us by providence. When God placed Adam and Eve in Paradise, He intended that they should work. Laziness is shameful! The greater our skill, whether innate or acquired, of working to capacity, the more perfectly we can fulfill God's designs; therein lies our perfection — the perfect fulfillment of the duties of our state.

But a sane and normal activity is one thing, and a feverish activity, another; one thing, the activity whose goal is the full accomplishment of the divine will, another, the activity whose aim is the mere satisfaction of a mania for movement even if nothing be achieved.

Speaking not only to religious but to all souls longing for divine union, Bossuet referred to the text which states that the vine must be pruned to bring forth the most fruit and exclaimed: "How many things must be pruned in you, O Christian! Do you wish to bear abundant fruit? Then it must cost you something. It is necessary to cut off this superfluous shoot, this branch which has grown out too far; you believe that you must be always active, always growing outward, and you become too exterior. . . . In the spring, when the vine begins to grow, it must be cut even to the flower if its growth is excessive."

Progress in Divine Union

These are wise words of counsel from an experienced guide. For is it not true that many souls desirous of recollection do not attain it at all, or at least not in the degree they would like, because of their feverish and moderate eagerness?

If to interior disquiet is added, as is often the case, the craving for exterior agitation, and the constantly satisfied desire of action for action's sake, there can be little hope for notable progress in divine union. God is not in the whirlwind. He does not care to communicate Himself in the midst of bustling noise.

Quite to the point here would be the gentle Latin reminder a Jesuit father addressed to those who, stimulated by the text they were reading aloud, read too rapidly, to the detriment of clear intelligibility: "*Pacate!* Read calmly!"

Oh, the precious adverb! Well might we hope that it would serve as a motto for many in their daily work and in their apostolate.

Not that we should neglect to put warmth and spirit into our endeavors, particularly in the service of our neighbor, but we should accomplish our work without agitation. "We accomplish no good without enthusiasm," said Lacordaire, and he was right. But enthusiasm is not feverishness. Many unfortunately confuse the two.

Develop union with God through prayer

How many individuals in their ordinary work, how many directors of activities in the exercise of their zeal become overeager and expend their energy with a nervous intensity that lacks control. Especially when they do it in the apostolate can the harm be universally recognized. Oh yes, there are many activities, much publicity, many books read, many ideas set in motion, many visits paid and received, many meetings held and sermons given, many study clubs, projects in abundance and to spare, works without number begun, and yet very little fruit as the result; much air beaten, but very little breath of the Holy Spirit. God is not in the whirlwind. And as in the case of the prophet, where a fruitful breeze would have been helpful, a tempestuous wind let loose — tempestuous and withering. The harvest is gathered, but there is no fruit.

Msgr. Dupanloup in his yearly retreat notes used to lament his inability to regulate his apostolic zeal, which led him into a consuming activity. Zealous he certainly was; he took no thought of self. Bishop of a large diocese, government representative, convention orator, and writer, he drew on immense resources to conquer souls. But he reproached himself with not having made a judicious use of these resources; he allowed them to engross him. And similarly Msgr. d'Hulst, rector of the Catholic Institute at Paris, preacher at Notre Dame, government representative, and spiritual director of many interior souls, admitted that on certain days he felt himself overwhelmed with occupations. He found it necessary to curb them; for the activity, in spite of himself, got the mastery over him.

There are two extremes. There are those who, be it said to their shame, do nothing, even when the distress of souls is great; and there are others who try to do too much or who throw themselves with frenzy into what they do.

Let us be active, yes, if possible, very active, but calmly, under the eye of God, only for His glory and with sufficient good sense to forbid ourselves whatever might impede our life of union, our prayer, and our spirit of prayer which alone can fructify our activity and zeal.

In practice, it is not always easy to know where to begin and where to stop. A mother of four young children writes, "I try to moderate my solicitude, but it gets the better of me. I feel that I must control it. God calls me often. Rarely do I consent to listen. There is always something to be put in order, a cupboard to inspect, an article of clothing to be mended. I could very well postpone these things, it is true, but it's too much for me. I know I ought to take time for prayer, but no, I must hasten to my cupboards and my many little duties. My prayer, short enough as it is, is often in grave danger. What can I do?"

What can we do? We ought to draw up for ourselves a rule of life that allots to prayer a fixed time that is in keeping with our state of life and the guidance of a spiritual director, and then we should hold fast to this time for prayer unless something urgent and unforeseen demands our dutiful attention, which we must give without any scruple. Elisabeth Leseur, who had achieved a high degree of divine union, used to interrupt her prayer immediately when her husband called her for a collar button or a pair of socks.

We should, if possible, plan our days so that by foresight we can avoid the crowding of our duties; to manage is to foresee. Naturally in our lives, but particularly if we are living in the world, there will be numerous unexpected happenings. We should try to foresee them or at least to foresee their possible or probable intervention and make provision for them. When we have done that, we should not try to accomplish in one hour the work of three, nor be downhearted if with the best of will we may be forced to postpone until tomorrow a task that seems very urgent and that we had planned to do today. No one expects us to do the impossible.

Besides, if we observe interior silence to the extent that circumstances permit, and force ourselves to live in God; if, while aiming at maximum activity that is also sincerely and vigorously controlled, we avoid feverishness; if we mercilessly deny ourselves useless interior and exterior chatter, we shall be surprised at time's almost unlimited power to expand.

It is unbelievable what some can accomplish while others, under the pretext of not having time, do nothing. Individuals who do not have a minute to spare, succeed, by a good beginning, in finding all the minutes they want. To have a great deal of time is not so important as to use well the little time we have. People who accomplish a vast amount of work are usually those who have not a minute to themselves, but who, despite swiftly passing time, remain calm and snatch from the fleeting moments their full power of achievement.

We also ought to resist the desire to be always doing something, to be active for activity's sake. Some occupations are detrimental. It might be better if the mother, of whom we spoke before, yielded to the divine attractions that urged her to withdraw into her soul, rather than to straighten for the tenth time a cupboard that was always already sufficiently orderly.

Develop union with God through prayer

Let us beware of the saying: "I always have something to do." That is often true, but it must be remembered that there is a hierarchy in things to be done. It is only reasonable that the most important should be first. At times it may be profitable to omit something, especially if the omission safeguards liberty of spirit and perfection of union. We should act with deliberation on the conviction that our many contacts with God during the day are not to be considered among the least profitable of our actions.

Let us beware, too, of the other saying: "I am not doing anything when I pray." The inactivity is only apparent. To pray is to do a great work, and the same holds true for every single instance, however brief, in which the soul plunges itself in God during the course of its manifold duties. Let us counteract the dictates of nature by a clear concept of faith.

We say "an act of the presence of God, an act of love of God." How could we claim that this is not acting? According to the absolute standard of values, it is the most beautiful act that can be made, and because God requires no other activity, it ought to be considered the most important. To live in truth helps tremendously to live in love.

Progress in Divine Union

It must be understood that the loving effort to be with God habitually, at each conscious breath of the soul, is not to be thought of as a strenuous intellectual effort, as an overwhelming preoccupation. In this case, a certain theoretical better may be the worst enemy of good enough. There is no use trying to be an angel. We are just poor human beings. It takes long practice in the cultivation of the interior life to achieve any noticeable result, and this result will always fall short of the ideal dreamed of by most souls. Striving souls must practice great patience. We do not find God by straining our nerves; we must have a sound method (such as we have tried to present), an increasing development of the spirit of faith, an untiring perseverance, and the wisdom that takes time into consideration.

For those who are too presumptuous or too eager to double the rate of their progress, Fr. Petitot closes his book *Introduction to Holiness* with an apt quotation from the great Dominican Tauler: "Whatever we do, try as we may, we shall never arrive at true peace, that peace which culminates in perfect union with God, before we are forty. . . ." And to quell imprudent ardor and inexperienced zeal he adds, "we must then wait ten years more before we are granted the Holy Spirit, the Comforter, the Spirit that teaches all things."

Develop union with God through prayer

We must understand what the passage means. Tauler did not pretend to limit the sanctifying powers of the Spirit of God, or to discourage beginners who are often more generous, more zealous, and more enthusiastic than the mature. We need only to think of the young saints: Stanislaus, Aloysius of Gonzaga, Rose of Lima, or Thérèse of the Child Jesus.[23] Age can be counted only by years, and the figures given by Tauler are like biblical figures; their meaning is rather symbolic than literal. Many, even pious people, go beyond forty or fifty years without reaching the degree of union attained by certain young people who determined at a very early age never to refuse God anything, and to develop a virile love.

The passage means, then, that the precious treasure is bought at a great price. We have no guarantee that a long period of time will in itself bring us to the heights of sanctity. Occasionally, for reasons of His own and perhaps to keep us humble, God permits us to struggle without

[23]St. Stanislaus Kostka (1550-1568), model Jesuit who died during his novitiate; St. Aloysius Gonzaga (1568-1591), young Jesuit who cared for plague victims; St. Rose of Lima (1586-1617), third order Dominican and first canonized saint of the Americas; St. Thérèse of Lisieux (1873-1897), Carmelite nun and Doctor famous for her "little way" of spirituality.

much noticeable gain, to make heroic efforts without ever knowing success.

The essential thing is not so much to reach our goal as to strive. In the spiritual life, more than anywhere else, "it is not the success which counts, but the effort." We make progress, if in spite of human frailties, we do not give up, but begin again each day where we left off the night before, even though we cannot detect any noticeable advancement. The divine word remains immutably true: "He who seeks finds." We would say, rather, "He who seeks has already found."

Chapter Nine

∞

*Never cease to progress
in union with God*

∞

To progress in divine union, we must never be satisfied to remain at a standstill. We must outdo ourselves; we must advance, cost what it may.

We never feel so small or so pitiable as when we endeavor to encourage others to heroic virtue. "But who are you, who speak to us, demanding generosity in sacrifice, effort, and perseverance in prayer? Without doubt you must be someone who practices consummate mortification and constant and ardent prayer."

Alas! But this is not the place for confession. What matters the person's worth if his counsels have intrinsic value? The apostle must often repeat the words of the Mass: "Lord, look not upon my sins, but upon the faith of Thy Church."

Do not judge him who has written this book, but pray for him.

One last reflection to leave with you, a thought from the works of Georges Duhamel that strangely moves the author of these pages each time he recalls it: "The man who stops for a second may stop for all eternity."

Stagnate, fall back, or advance?

What do you want to do?

Fall back?

Oh! no.

Stop? Remain where you are?

No, not that either.

Progress? All right! Then begin.

Biographical Note

∞

Raoul Plus, S.J.

(1882-1958)

∞

Raoul Plus was born in Boulogne-sur-Mer, France, where he attended the Jesuit college. In 1899 he entered the Jesuit novitiate in Amiens and was ordained there. Because of laws that persecuted religious orders at that time, Fr. Plus had to leave France in 1901 and did not return from this exile for ten years, during which time he studied literature, philosophy, and theology in Belgium and Holland. He also taught courses in the field of humanities.

At the advent of World War I, Fr. Plus enlisted as a soldier, and subsequently as chaplain, and later was awarded the Croix de Guerre and the Medaille Militaire for his heroism. It was during this time that he began to write, producing his first two books, which were followed by a host of works on various aspects of the spiritual life, and in particular, about the presence of Christ in the soul.

After the war, Fr. Plus taught religion at the Catholic Institute of Arts and Sciences in Lille and became a well-loved spiritual director for the students. During school vacations, he gave retreats for priests and seminarians and wrote several books about priests.

In his lifetime, Fr. Plus wrote more than forty books aimed at helping Catholics understand God's loving relationship with the soul. His words consistently stress the vital role of prayer in the spiritual life and seek to show how to live out important spiritual truths. His direct, practical style renders his works invaluable for those seeking to know Christ better and to develop a closer union with Him in their souls.

∞

Sophia Institute Press®

∞

Sophia Institute® is a nonprofit institution that seeks to restore man's knowledge of eternal truth, including man's knowledge of his own nature, his relation to other persons, and his relation to God.

Sophia Institute Press® serves this end in numerous ways: it publishes translations of foreign works to make them accessible to English-speaking readers; it brings out-of-print books back into print; and it publishes important new books that fulfill the ideals of Sophia Institute®. These books afford readers a rich source of the enduring wisdom of mankind.

Sophia Institute Press® makes these high-quality books available to the general public by using advanced technology and by soliciting donations to subsidize its general publishing costs.

Your generosity can help Sophia Institute Press® to provide the public with handsome editions of works containing the enduring wisdom of the ages. Please send your tax-deductible contribution to the address below. We also welcome your questions, comments, and suggestions.

For your free catalog, call:
Toll-free: 1-800-888-9344

or write:
Sophia Institute Press®
Box 5284
Manchester, NH 03108

or visit our website:
www.sophiainstitute.com

Sophia Institute® is a tax-exempt institution
as defined by the Internal Revenue Code,
Section 501(c)(3). Tax I.D. 22-2548708.